HTMX Crash Course
Extend HTML with
Simple yet Powerful Code

Greg Lim

First Edition: May 2024

Table of Contents

Preface

In this book, we take you on a fun, hands-on crash course to learning HTMX. You'll start building your first app with HTMX within minutes. Every section is written in a bite-sized manner and straight to the point as I don't want to waste your time (and most certainly mine) on the content you don't need.

In the course of this book, we will cover:
- Chapter 1: Introduction to HTMX
- Chapter 2: BMI Calculator
- Chapter 3: Polling – Bitcoin Price Tracker App
- Chapter 4: Building a Search Widget
- Chapter 5: Form Inline Validation
- Chapter 6: Show Edit Form and Update

The goal of this book is to teach you HTMX in a manageable way without overwhelming you. We focus only on the essentials and cover the material in a hands-on practice manner for you to code along.

Getting Book Updates

To receive updated versions of the book, subscribe to our mailing list by sending a mail to support@i-ducate.com. I try to update my books to use the latest version of software, libraries and will update the codes/content in this book. So do subscribe to my list to receive updated copies!

Contact and Code Examples

Contact me at support@i-ducate.com to obtain the source files used in this book. Comments or questions concerning this book can also be directed to the same.

Online Course Version

If you are a more visual learner and learn better from absorbing this book's content through an online course, you can get access to the book's online course version free by contacting support@i-ducate.com and providing a proof of purchase.

Chapter 1: Introduction to HTMX

In this short book, we're going to be looking at and experimenting with htmx. It's a small JavaScript library that allows us to create dynamic front ends without having to write any JavaScript at all. We can do this using special attributes in our HTML called hyperscript attributes.

For e.g., we can make HTTP requests by adding in a specific attribute. In the HTMX documentation home page (htmx.org/), we have a button with an *hx-post* attribute:

quick start

```
<script src="https://unpkg.com/htmx.org@1.9.12"></script>
<!-- have a button POST a click via AJAX -->
<button hx-post="/clicked" hx-swap="outerHTML">
  Click Me
</button>
```

The `hx-post` and `hx-swap` attributes on this button tell htmx:

> "When a user clicks on this button, issue an AJAX request to /clicked, and replace the entire button with the HTML response"

When the button is clicked, a post request is made to the '/clicked' endpoint. The *hx-swap* attribute takes the response and swap this button with the response from the backend. We will illustrate more on *hx-post* and *hs-swap* later.

Under 'motivation' in the documentation:

motivation

- Why should only `<a>` & `<form>` be able to make HTTP requests?

- Why should only `click` & `submit` events trigger them?

- Why should only `GET` & `POST` methods be available?

- Why should you only be able to replace the **entire** screen?

By removing these constraints, htmx completes HTML as a hypertext

Traditionally when you create a form and submit to a server, you can only do GET or POST requests, but with HTMX, you can use PUT, PATCH, DELETE with *hx-put*, *hx-patch* and *hx-delete* attributes respectively.

You can also make HTTP requests using any element, not just <a> tags and <form> tags.

What we're going to do

We're going to use Node and Express as our backend, but it could be anything. Eg. HTMX is popular with Django and Golang, but you could have anything as your backend. We'll be using Node and Express in this book.

HTMX is small sized, only 14 kilobytes:

htmx is small (~14k min.gz'd), dependency-free, extendable, IE11 compatible & has **reduced** code base sizes by 67% when compared with react

So, it's very lightweight. If you want dynamic functionality like easily make requests and replace certain parts of your application without having the page reload, and don't want to use front end frameworks like React or Vue, HTMX is a great option.

HTMX Attributes

If we look under *Reference* (htmx.org/reference/), you'll see the different attributes available eg. *hx-get* and *hx-post* to make GET and POST requests:

Core Attribute Reference

The most common attributes when using htmx.

Attribute	Description
hx-get	issues a GET to the specified URL
hx-post	issues a POST to the specified URL
hx-on*	handle events with inline scripts on elements
hx-push-url	push a URL into the browser location bar to create history
hx-select	select content to swap in from a response

You also have *hx-delete*:

Additional Attribute Reference

All other attributes available in htmx.

Attribute	Description
hx-boost	add progressive enhancement for links and forms
hx-confirm	shows a confirm() dialog before issuing a request
hx-delete	issues a DELETE to the specified URL

And PUT and PATCH:

hx-patch	issues a PATCH to the specified URL
hx-preserve	specifies elements to keep unchanged between requests
hx-prompt	shows a prompt() before submitting a request
hx-put	issues a PUT to the specified URL

We also have *hx-swap*:

hx-swap	controls how content will swap in (outerHTML , beforeend , afterend , ...)

If you don't want to just swap/replace the element that's making the request with the response, but want to target somewhere else, you could use *hx-target*:

hx-target	specifies the target element to be swapped

hx-trigger is used to specify the event that triggers the request:

hx-trigger	specifies the event that triggers the request

Eg. if you want to send a HTTP request on a click or a mouseover, or any other event, you can specify using *hx-trigger*.

Now let's go through some small projects to concretely show how to apply the above, use HTMX as our front end with a simple Node.js and Express server on our backend.

Setting Up our Simple Node.js and Express Backend

We're going to set up a basic server with a 'public' directory to serve HTML files containing htmx attributes.

If you aren't familiar with Node and Express, I have published a book on it. Contact me at support@i-ducate.com for a copy.

Ensure you have Node.js installed. Go to nodejs.org, download Node, install it, and you should have access to the node command. Run the below command in your Terminal:
```
node -v
```

and you should get the Node version logged:
```
(base) MacBook-Air-2:~ user$ node -v
v20.6.1
```

Next in the Terminal, go to your folder of choice and generate a package.json, by running:
```
npm init -y
```

That will create our package.json file. Next, install *express* by running:

```
npm i express
```

We also want to install as a dev-dependency *nodemon* to continuously watch our server file so we don't have to restart the server when there are code changes. Run:

```
npm i -D nodemon
```

In package.json, let's add two things. To use *import* over the *require* syntax, add in **bold**:
```
{
  "name": "htmx",
  "version": "1.0.0",
  "description": "",
  "main": "index.js",
  "type": "module",
  "scripts": {
    "dev": "nodemon server.js"
  },
  "keywords": [],
  "author": "",
  ...
  ...
}
```

We also create a *dev* script to run our server.js with nodemon.

server.js

Let's next create our server.js:

server.js is the entry point to our backend. Add in the below codes into server.js:

```
import express from 'express';

const app = express();

// Set static folder
app.use(express.static('public'));

// Parse URL-encoded bodies (as sent by HTML forms)
app.use(express.urlencoded ({ extended: true }));

// Parse JSON bodies (as sent by API clients)
app.use(express.json());

// Start the server
app.listen (3000, ()=>{
     console. log('Server listening on port 3000');
});
```

Code Explanation

```
import express from 'express';

const app = express();
```

We bring in *express*, initializing it into the *app* variable. We then have a couple of lines of middleware.

```
app.use(express.static('public'));
```

This makes the *public* folder static so we can serve HTML files from it.

```
// Parse URL-encoded bodies (as sent by HTML forms)
app.use(express.urlencoded ({ extended: true }));

// Parse JSON bodies (as sent by API clients)
app.use(express.json());
```

The above two lines are middleware to get data from JSON API clients and form bodies.

```
app.listen (3000, ()=>{
  console. log('Server listening on port 3000');
});
```

Lastly, we start the server on port 3000.

Running our App

In Terminal, run:

```
npm run dev
```

And the server is listening on port 3000:

```
(base) MacBook-Air-2:htmx user$ npm run dev

> htmx@1.0.0 dev
> nodemon server.js

[nodemon] 3.1.0
[nodemon] to restart at any time, enter `rs`
[nodemon] watching path(s): *.*
[nodemon] watching extensions: js,mjs,cjs,json
[nodemon] starting `node server.js`
Server listening on port 3000
```

Currently, we haven't created any routes yet. So there's nothing to hit or go to, but our server is up and running.

'public' folder

Let's create a folder called *public* where all our HTML files will go.

In *public*, create a index.html file with a simple html:

12

```
<!DOCTYPE html>
<html lang="en">
<head>
    <meta charset="UTF-8">
    <meta name="viewport" content="width=device-width, …">
    <title>Hello World</title>
</head>
<body>
    <h1>Hello World!</h1>
    <p>Welcome to my website.</p>
</body>
</html>
```

Because we have made *public* folder static, we should be able to go to localhost:3000 and see index.html:

Hello World!

Welcome to my website.

Get Started with HTMX

To install HTMX, there's a couple of ways to do it. If we go to htmx.org/docs/#installing, you can download it locally and include it in your file structure or you can install it with *npm* if you're using front end tooling:

Download a copy

The next easiest way to install htmx is to simply copy it into your project.

Download `htmx.min.js` from unpkg.com and add it to the appropriate directory in your project and include it where necessary with a `<script>` tag:

```
<script src="/path/to/htmx.min.js"></script>
```

You can also add extensions this way, by downloading them from the `ext/` directory.

npm

For npm-style build systems, you can install htmx via npm:

```
npm install htmx.org
```

After installing, you'll need to use appropriate tooling to use `node_modules/htmx.org/dist/htmx.js` (or `.min.js`). For example, you might bundle htmx with some extensions and project-specific code.

13

However, the easiest way to install is via CDN. Let's do this:

Via A CDN (e.g. unpkg.com)

The fastest way to get going with htmx is to load it via a CDN. You can simply add this to your head tag and get going:

```
<script src="https://unpkg.com/htmx.org@1.9.12" integrity="sha384-ujb
```

Unminified version is also available

```
<script src="https://unpkg.com/htmx.org@1.9.12/dist/htmx.js" integrit
```

While the CDN approach is extremely simple, you may want to consider not using CDNs in production.

Grab the *script* tag:

```
<script src="https://unpkg.com/htmx.org@1.9.12" integrity="sha384-…"
crossorigin="anonymous"></script>
```

Put that in the <head> tag (shown in **bold**):

```
<!DOCTYPE html>
<html lang="en">
<head>
    <meta charset="UTF-8">
    <meta name="viewport" content="width=device-width, initial-
scale=1.0">
    <script
        src="https://unpkg.com/htmx.org@1.9.12"
        integrity="sha384-…"
        crossorigin="anonymous">
    </script>
    <title>Hello World</title>
</head>
<body>
…
…
```

In addition, let's add Bootstrap (getbootstrap.com/docs/5.3/getting-started/introduction/) to make our app look nice. So add the <link> tag in <head>, and <script> tag before the closing </body>:

2. **Include Bootstrap's CSS and JS.** Place the `<link>` tag in the `<head>` for our CSS, and the `<script>` tag for our JavaScript bundle (including Popper for positioning dropdowns, poppers, and tooltips) before the closing `</body>`. Learn more about our CDN links.

```html
<!doctype html>
<html lang="en">
  <head>
    <meta charset="utf-8">
    <meta name="viewport" content="width=device-width, initial-scale=1">
    <title>Bootstrap demo</title>
    <link href="https://cdn.jsdelivr.net/npm/bootstrap@5.3.3/dist/css/bootstrap.min
  </head>
  <body>
    <h1>Hello, world!</h1>
    <script src="https://cdn.jsdelivr.net/npm/bootstrap@5.3.3/dist/js/bootstrap.bun
  </body>
</html>
```

In index.html, it will look something like:

```html
...
<head>
    <meta charset="UTF-8">
    <meta name="viewport" content="width=device-width, initial-scale=1.0">
    <script
        src="https://unpkg.com/htmx.org@1.9.12"
        ...
    </script>
    <title>Hello World</title>
    <link
href="https://cdn.jsdelivr.net/npm/bootstrap@5.3.3/dist/css/bootstrap.min.css" rel="stylesheet" integrity="sha384-… " crossorigin="anonymous">
</head>
<body>
    <h1>Hello World!</h1>
    <script
src="https://cdn.jsdelivr.net/npm/bootstrap@5.3.3/dist/js/bootstrap.bundle.min.js" integrity="sha384-…" crossorigin="anonymous"></script>
</body>
</html>
```

If we reload the page now, the font should change. So we know Bootstrap is included.

Hello World!

Button to Make Request and Receive Response

First, let's see how a button can make a request and get that response without any JavaScript, just by using HTMX attributes.

In the body, add the code in **bold**:

```
...
<body>
    <div class="container">
        <h1>Simple Request Example</h1>
        <button type="button" class="btn btn-primary">
            Fetch Some Stuff
        </button>
    </div>
    <script ...></script>
</body>
...
```

We have a button with the text "Fetch Some Stuff".

Simple Request Example

Fetch Some Stuff

We use a public API, like JSONPlaceholder (https://jsonplaceholder.typicode.com/) to fetch some fake users:

```
←  →  C    jsonplaceholder.typicode.com/users
```

Pretty print ☐

```
[
  {
    "id": 1,
    "name": "Leanne Graham",
    "username": "Bret",
    "email": "Sincere@april.biz",
    "address": {
      "street": "Kulas Light",
      "suite": "Apt. 556",
      "city": "Gwenborough",
      "zipcode": "92998-3874",
      "geo": {
        "lat": "-37.3159",
        "lng": "81.1496"
      }
    },
    "phone": "1-770-736-8031 x56442",
    "website": "hildegard.org",
    "company": {
      "name": "Romaguera-Crona",
      "catchPhrase": "Multi-layered client-server neural-net",
      "bs": "harness real-time e-markets"
    }
  },
```

hs-get

In the button, we send a GET request with *hx-get*:

```
<body>
    <div class="container">
        <h1>Simple Request Example</h1>
        <button
            hx-get="https://jsonplaceholder.typicode.com/users"
            hx-trigger="click"
            class="btn btn-primary"
        >
            Fetch Some Stuff
        </button>
    </div>
    ...
    ...
```

In *hx-get*, we put the URL we want to make the GET request to. That will give me an array of users. In addition, we include *hx-trigger* and specify the 'click' event request i.e., the button sends the GET request when the button is clicked.

So if we click "Fetch Some Stuff", it makes the request, receives the JSON array response, and puts it in the button.

Note: if this doesn't work for you, you might be getting an "button: htmx:invalidPath" error. This is due to HTMX introducing the config flag *htmx.config.selfRequestsOnly* which defaults to True and doesn't allow making requests to URLs not on the same origin page. Thus, we have to add the below:

```
<head>
    ...
    <script src="https://unpkg.com/htmx.org@2.0.3" integrity="..."></script>
    <script>
        htmx.config.selfRequestsOnly = false;
    </script>
    <title>Hello World</title>
    ...
</head>
```

And when you run your apps, the request should work:

Simple Request Example

[{ "id": 1, "name": "Leanne Graham", "username": "Bret", "email": "Sincere@april.biz", "address": { "street": "Kulas Light", "suite": "Apt. 556", "city": "Gwenborough", "zipcode": "92998-3874", "geo": { "lat": "-37.3159", "lng": "81.1496" } }, "phone": "1-770-736-8031 x56442", "website": "hildegard.org", "company": { "name": "Romaguera-Crona", "catchPhrase": "Multi-layered client-server neural-net", "bs": "harness real-time e-markets" } }, { "id": 2, "name": "Ervin Howell", "username": "Antonette", "email": "Shanna@melissa.tv", "address": { "street": "Victor Plains", "suite": "Suite 879", "city": "Wisokyburgh", "zipcode": "90566-7771", "geo": { "lat": "-43.9509", "lng": "-34.4618" } }, "phone": "010-692-6593 x09125", "website": "anastasia.net", "company": { "name": "Deckow-Crist", "catchPhrase": "Proactive didactic contingency", "bs": "synergize scalable supply-chains" } }, { "id": 3, "name": "Clementine Bauch", "username": "Samantha", "email": "Nathan@yesenia.net", "address": { "street": "Douglas Extension", "suite": "Suite 847", "city": "McKenziehaven", "zipcode": "59590-4157", "geo": { "lat": "-68.6102", "lng": "-47.0653" } }, "phone": "1-463-123-4447", "website": "ramiro.info", "company": { "name": "Romaguera-Jacobson", "catchPhrase": "Face to face bifurcated interface", "bs": "e-enable strategic applications" } }, { "id": 4, "name": "Patricia Lebsack", "username": "Karianne", "email": "Julianne.OConner@kory.org", "address": { "street": "Hoeger Mall", "suite": "Apt. 692", "city": "South Elvis", "zipcode": "53919-4257", "geo": { "lat": "29.4572", "lng": "-164.2990" } }, "phone": "493-170-9623 x156", "website": "kale.biz", "company": { "name": "Robel-Corkery", "catchPhrase": "Multi-tiered zero tolerance productivity", "bs": "transition cutting-edge web services" } }, { "id": 5, "name": "Chelsey Dietrich", "username": "Kamren", "email": "Lucio_Hettinger@annie.ca", "address": { "street": "Skiles Walks", "suite": "Suite 351", "city": "Roscoeview", "zipcode": "33263", "geo": { "lat": "-31.8129", "lng": "62.5342" } }, "phone": "(254)954-1289", "website": "demarco.info", "company": { "name": "Keebler LLC", "catchPhrase": "User-centric fault-tolerant solution", "bs": "revolutionize end-to-end systems" } }, { "id": 6, "name": "Mrs. Dennis Schulist", "username": "Leopoldo_Corkery", "email":

We end up with a giant button because we didn't specify any target where we want the response data (we will address this later).

Now we actually don't need the hx-trigger='click':

```
<button
    hx-get="https://jsonplaceholder.typicode.com/users"
    hx-trigger="click"
    class="btn btn-primary"
>
```

because that's the default for a button. But if we wanted something different, eg. a mouseover event to make the request, we can specify:

```
<button
    hx-get="https://jsonplaceholder.typicode.com/users"
    hx-trigger="mouseover"
    class="btn btn-primary"
>
```

So you're not bound to certain events to make requests.

hx-swap

Currently, the response data received is placed inside the button which shouldn't be the case. Let's look at *hx-swap* which allows us to swap out the button for the response.

Add in **bold**:

```
<button
    hx-get="https://jsonplaceholder.typicode.com/users"
    hx-swap="outerHTML"
    class="btn btn-primary"
>
    Fetch Some Stuff
</button>
```

Now, if I click the button, you'll see the button goes away, and the button is replaced with the response:

Simple Request Example

[{ "id": 1, "name": "Leanne Graham", "username": "Bret", "email": "Sincere@april.biz", "address": { "street": "Kulas Light", "suite": "Apt. 556", "city": "Gwenborough", "zipcode": "92998-3874", "geo": { "lat": "-37.3159", "lng": "81.1496" } }, "phone": "1-770-736-8031 x56442", "website": "hildegard.org", "company": { "name": "Romaguera-Crona", "catchPhrase": "Multi-layered client-server neural-net", "bs": "harness real-time e-markets" } }, { "id": 2, "name": "Ervin Howell", "username": "Antonette", "email": "Shanna@melissa.tv", "address": { "street": "Victor Plains", "suite": "Suite 879", "city": "Wisokyburgh", "zipcode": "90566-7771", "geo": { "lat": "-43.9509", "lng": "-34.4618" } }, "phone": "010-692-6593 x09125", "website": "anastasia.net", "company": { "name": "Deckow-Crist", "catchPhrase": "Proactive didactic contingency", "bs": "synergize scalable supply-chains" } }, { "id": 3, "name": "Clementine Bauch", "username": "Samantha", "email": "Nathan@yesenia.net", "address": { "street": "Douglas Extension", "suite": "Suite 847", "city": "McKenziehaven", "zipcode": "59590-4157", "geo": { "lat": "-68.6102", "lng": "-47.0653" } }, "phone": "1-463-123-4447", "website":

hx-swap can take selectors like outerHTML, innerHTML and others:

hx-swap

The `hx-swap` attribute allows you to specify how the response will be swapped in relative to the target of an AJAX request. If you do not specify the option, the default is `htmx.config.defaultSwapStyle` (`innerHTML`).

The possible values of this attribute are:

- `innerHTML` - Replace the inner html of the target element
- `outerHTML` - Replace the entire target element with the response
- `beforebegin` - Insert the response before the target element
- `afterbegin` - Insert the response before the first child of the target element
- `beforeend` - Insert the response after the last child of the target element
- `afterend` - Insert the response after the target element
- `delete` - Deletes the target element regardless of the response
- `none` - Does not append content from response (out of band items will still be processed).

(https://htmx.org/attributes/hx-swap/)

We just used outerHTML which replaces the target element (in this case, the button) with the response.

Now, we should not be showing the JSON direct, but replace it with a HTML list of users which we will illustrate soon.

Request from our own API

Currently, we are showing user data from a third party API, let's illustrate next, how to request to our own API.

Replace the JSON placeholder link with just '/users'. Change in **bold**:

```
<button
    hx-get="/users"
    hx-swap="outerHTML"
    class="btn btn-primary"
>
```

Since there's no domain name, it will look at our own server.

When you click on the button, and look under Developer console, you'll see it is making a request:

We get a 404 because the *users* endpoint doesn't yet exist.

Let's create that in server.js where we will put all our routes. Add into server.js:
...
...

```
app.use(express.json());

// Handle GET request to fetch users
app.get('/users', (req, res) => {
    const users = [
        { id: 1, name: 'John Doe' },
        { id: 2, name: 'Bob Williams' },
        { id: 3, name: 'Shannon Jackson'},
    ]

    res.send(`
        <h2>Users</h2>
        <ul class="list-group">
            ${users.map((user)=>`<li class="list-group-
item">${user.name}</li>`).join('')}
        </ul>
    `)
});

app.listen (3000, ()=>{
  console.log('Server listening on port 3000');
});
```

Code Explanation

```
// Handle GET request to fetch users
app.get('/users', (req, res) => {
```

We handle the GET request to fetch users with a callback function that takes in request and response objects.

```
const users = [
        { id: 1, name: 'John Doe' },
        { id: 2, name: 'Bob Williams' },
        { id: 3, name: 'Shannon Jackson'},
]
```

For now, we just have a static array of users. Later, we will show how we can get users from the JSONPlaceholder API.

```
    res.send(`
        <h2>Users</h2>
        <ul class="list-group">
            ${users.map((user)=>`<li class="list-group-item">
                ${user.name}</li>`).join('')}
        </ul>
    `)
```

We then use our response object *res*, which has a method *send*, and in it, use back ticks ` for a template string, where we *map* through the users and output a list item for each user.

Because we're taking an array and using *map*, we add *.join(")* to turn it to a string.

Running our App

Let's save that and run it. And when I click 'Fetch Some Stuff', we get our users in a list:

Simple Request Example

Users

John Doe

Bob Williams

Shannon Jackson

To reiterate, although we are using Node and Express, you could do this with other backends like Django. And in our frontend, we have no JavaScript at all. We just added *hx* attributes.

hx-target

Currently, when we click the button, the response replaces it. You probably want to put that somewhere else rather than replacing the button.

With *hx-target*, we can target a certain element id to put the response in:

```html
<div class="container">
    <h1>Simple Request Example</h1>
    <button
        hx-get="/users"
        hx-target="#users"
        class="btn btn-primary"
    >
        Fetch Some Stuff
    </button>

    <div id="users"></div>
</div>
```

For eg, in the button, I specify *hx-target="#users"*. The response will then be placed in the *div* with *id='users'*:

23

Simple Request Example

Fetch Some Stuff

Users

John Doe

Bob Williams

Shannon Jackson

hx-confirm

We can also show a confirmation box using *hx-confirm*. Eg:

```
<button
    hx-get="/users"
    hx-target="#users"
    hx-confirm="Do you want to proceed with fetching users?"
    class="btn btn-primary"
>
    Fetch Some Stuff
</button>
```

And when we click the button, we get:

So if you're making a delete request or other critical decisions, this would be helpful.

Getting Data from API

Currently, we are getting from a hardcoded array of users. Let's change it to get from the JSONplaceholder API. Make the code changes in **bold**:

```
app.get('/users', async (req, res) => {
    const users = [
        { id: 1, name: 'John Doe' },
        { id: 2, name: 'Bob Williams' },
        { id: 3, name: 'Shannon Jackson'},
    ]

    const response = await
fetch('https://jsonplaceholder.typicode.com/users')
    const users = await response.json()

    res.send(`
        <h2>Users</h2>
        <ul class="list-group">
            ${users.map((user)=>`<li class="list-group-
item">${user.name}</li>`).join('')}
        </ul>
    `)
});
```

Code Explanation

```
app.get('/users', async (req, res) => {
  const response = await
fetch('https://jsonplaceholder.typicode.com/users')
    const users = await response.json()
```

Since I'm going making a *fetch* request and using *await*, I'm going to add *async* to the callback function. We then await and fetch from JSONPlaceholder. From that response, we want the JSON.

The rest of the code where we loop through and output the names doesn't change.

Running our App

Let's save that, reload, and click 'Fetch some Stuff', and we get the users from the API.

Simple Request Example

Fetch Some Stuff

Users

Leanne Graham

Ervin Howell

Clementine Bauch

Patricia Lebsack

Chelsey Dietrich

Mrs. Dennis Schulist

Kurtis Weissnat

Nicholas Runolfsdottir V

Glenna Reichert

Clementina DuBuque

Send Data with your Request

When you want to send data with your request, we can do that with *hx-vals*. For eg. in the JSONPlaceholder API, we can specify a limit on the number of results by adding:

`https://jsonplaceholder.typicode.com/users?_limit=1`

Let's add *hx-vals* to our button and specify a JSON object with the value and key in it. Add the below in **bold**:

```
<button
    hx-get="/users"
    hx-target="#users"
    hx-vals='{"limit":3}'
    class="btn btn-primary"
>
    Fetch Some Stuff
</button>
```

So, we pass a JSON object with a key 'limit' and value of 3.

Back in our server.js backend, we add:

```
app.get('/users', async (req, res) => {
  const limit = +req.query.limit || 10;

  const response = await fetch('https://jsonplaceholder.typicode.com/users')
  ...
```

We retrieve the value with *req.query.limit* and add a '+' sign to convert it from a string to a number. And if *limit* doesn't exist, we assign the default of 10.

Next in the fetching from the JSON Placeholder API, we add a query string of limit and set it to the value you want. Add in **bold**:

```
app.get('/users', async (req, res) => {
    const limit = +req.query.limit || 10;

    const response = await fetch(
        `https://jsonplaceholder.typicode.com/users?_limit=${limit}`
    );
  ...
```

Note that we change the quotes "" to backticks `.We append and set *limit* to *_limit*. Remember that we get *limit* from the *hx-val* attribute in the button in index.html:

```
        <button
            hx-get="/users"
            hx-target="#users"
            hx-vals='{"limit":3}'
            class="btn btn-primary"
        >
```

Running our App

Now when I fetch users, I get only three users because we send the *limit* of '3' to the back end through the *hx-val* attribute.

Simple Request Example

Fetch Some Stuff

Users

Leanne Graham

Ervin Howell

Clementine Bauch

hx-indicator

The *hx-indicator* attribute allows you to load a loading or spinner graphic or whatever you want while it's waiting for the server. To illustrate, in index.html, add the *hx-indicator* attribute to the element you want to show when it's interacting with the server.

```
<body>
    <div class="container">
        <h1>Simple Request Example</h1>
        <button
            hx-get="/users"
            hx-target="#users"
            hx-vals='{"limit":3}'
            hx-indicator="#loading"
            class="btn btn-primary"
        >
            Fetch Some Stuff
        </button>
        ...
```

Let's next add a spinner component from Bootstrap (https://getbootstrap.com/docs/4.2/components/spinners/):

```
...
    <div class="container">
        <h1>Simple Request Example</h1>
        <button
            hx-get="/users"
            hx-target="#users"
            hx-vals='{"limit":3}'
            hx-indicator="#loading"
```

28

```
        class="btn btn-primary"
    >
        Fetch Some Stuff
    </button>

    <div id="loading" class="htmx-indicator spinner-border"
        role="status">
    </div>
    <div id="users"></div>
</div>
...
```

Note: we specify an id of "loading" in the spinner (reference to "#loading" in the button) and also the *htmx-indicator* in the class attribute.

Currently, you might not see the spinner after clicking on 'Fetch some stuff' as it disappears quickly. We can mimic a slower server by using *setTimeout* and waiting two seconds. Add the codes in **bold**:

```
app.get('/users', async (req, res) => {
    setTimeout(async ()=> {
        const limit = +req.query.limit || 10;

        const response = await fetch(
            `https://jsonplaceholder.typicode.com/users?_limit=${limit}`
        );
        const users = await response.json()

        res.send(`
            <h2>Users</h2>
            <ul class="list-group">
                ${users.map((user)=>`<li class="list-group-
item">${user.name}</li>`).join('')}
            </ul>
        `)
    },2000)
});
```

Essentially, we wrap the code with *setTimeout* that takes in a function, and we specify to wait 2000 milliseconds (two seconds).

Let's reload and click the button. Now it's waiting two seconds and you can see it shows the indicator as it waits:

Simple Request Example

Chapter 2: BMI Calculator

Let's begin a new project. If you've finished the previous chapter, you can copy the existing code in index.html and paste it in a fresh new index.html. Make sure the new index.html includes the HTMX and Bootstrap scripts:

```
<!DOCTYPE html>
<html lang="en">
<head>
    <meta charset="UTF-8">
    <meta name="viewport" content="width=device-width, initial-scale=1.0">
    <script  src="https://unpkg.com/htmx.org@1.9.12" …>
    </script>
    <title>Hello World</title>
    <link href="https://cdn.jsdelivr.net/npm/bootstrap@5.3.3/...>
</head>
<body>
    <div class="container">
        <h1>Simple Request Example</h1>
    </div>
    <script
src="https://cdn.jsdelivr.net/npm/bootstrap@5.3.3...></script>
</body>
</html>
```

Note: Contact support@i-ducate.com to get the sample codes for each chapter.

We will create a simple Body Mass Index (BMI) calculator where we pass in a body's height, weight and it gives us a BMI result back.

We will have a form that when submitted, goes to the backend to calculate the BMI and sends back some markup to show us the BMI.

In index.html, we add a form (getbootstrap.com/docs/5.3/forms/overview/). So we have a simple markup with no HTMX yet:

```html
<!DOCTYPE html>
<html lang="en">
<head>
      ...
</head>
<body>
    <div class="container">
        <h1>BMI Calculator</h1>
        <form>
            <input name="height" type="text" class="form-control"
                placeholder="Enter Height in Meters">
            <input name="weight" type="text" class="form-control"
                placeholder="Enter Weight in Kg">
            <button type="submit" class="btn btn-primary">
                Calculate BMI
            </button>
        </form>
    </div>

    <script ...></script>
</body>
</html>
```

This gives us:

BMI Calculator

Enter Height in Meters

Enter Weight in Kg

Calculate BMI

We have a form with two inputs, height and weight.

Next, add to the form in **bold**:

```html
    <form
        hx-trigger="submit"
        hx-post="/calculate"
        hx-target="#result"
    >
        <input name="height" type="text" class="form-control"
placeholder="Enter Height in Meters">
        <input name="weight" type="text" class="form-control"
placeholder="Enter Weight in Kg">
```

31

```
<button type="submit" class="btn btn-primary">
        Calculate BMI
</button>
<div id="result"></div>
</form>
```

Code Explanation

`hx-trigger="submit"`

To send the request, we add to the form *hx-trigger* and set that to *submit*. i.e. The form sends a request when we submit. In case you are wondering, this is actually the default for a form, so we don't really need to add *hx-trigger* here, but I'm adding it for teaching purposes.

`hx-post="/calculate"`

We want to send a POST request, so instead of *hx-get*, we do *hx-post*. We send the POST request to the */calculate* route in our backend.

```
<form
...
    hx-target="#result"
>
    <input name="height" ... >
    <input name="weight" ... >
    <button type="submit" class="btn btn-primary">
        Calculate BMI
    </button>
    <div id="result"></div>
</form>
```

Using *hx-target*, we place the response to the element of id *result*.

Calculate Endpoint

Let's next create the *calculate* endpoint in server.js.

In server.js, add:

```
...
app.get('/users', async (req, res) => {
    ...
});
```

```
app.post('/calculate',(req,res)=>{
    const height = parseFloat(req.body.height);
    const weight = parseFloat(req.body.weight);

    const bmi = weight/(height * height);

    res.send(`
        <p>Height of ${height} & Weight of ${weight} gives you BMI of
${bmi.toFixed(2)}</p>
        `);
})

app.listen (3000, ()=>{
    console.log('Server listening on port 3000');
});
```

Code Explanation

```
app.post('/calculate',(req,res)=>{
```

We handle the post request for BMI calculation with */calculate* as the endpoint.

```
    const height = parseFloat(req.body.height);
```

We retrieve height with *req.body.height* and parse it as a float.

If we look at the input in the form in index.html, it has the name of height:
```
<input name="height" type="text" class="form-control" placeholder="...">
```

Note that we can get data from the body with *req.body* because we have earlier added the middlewares:

```
app.use(express.urlencoded ({ extended: true }));
app.use(express.json());
```

We repeat the same for *weight*: `const weight = parseFloat(req.body.weight);`

```
    const bmi = weight/(height * height);
```

We enter the formula to calculate BMI.

```
    res.send(`
        <p>Height of ${height} & Weight of ${weight} gives you BMI of
${bmi.toFixed(2)}</p>
        `);
```

We then send back the response with *res.send*, we send back a template string and also add *.toFixed*(2) to round BMI to two decimal places.

Running our App

Let's save that. In our form, enter height, weight and get the BMI result:

BMI Calculator

1.7

80

Calculate BMI

Height of 1.7 and weight of 80 will give you a BMI of 27.68

You can of course add an if-else logic to determine if the BMI is in a healthy range or unhealthy range:

- **If your BMI is less than 18.5**, it falls within the underweight range.
- **If your BMI is 18.5 to 24.9**, it falls within the Healthy Weight range.
- **If your BMI is 25.0 to 29.9**, it falls within the overweight range.
- **If your BMI is 30.0 or higher**, it falls within the obese range.

(taken from www.cdc.gov/healthyweight/assessing/)

But that's beyond the scope of this book.

In this chapter, we showed how HTMX works with a form, using a different trigger (ie 'submit') and a POST request over a GET request.

Chapter 3: Polling – Bitcoin Price Tracker App

Let's next explore polling, where make a request to the server every so often (e.g. every five seconds or 30 seconds) to get updated data.

Save your index.html from the previous chapter and start a fresh new index.html:

```
<!DOCTYPE html>
<html lang="en">
<head>
    <meta charset="UTF-8">
    <meta name="viewport" content="width=device-width, initial-scale=1.0">
    <script
        src="https://unpkg.com/htmx.org@1.9.12" …>
    </script>
    <link href="https://cdn.jsdelivr.net/npm/bootstrap@5.3.3/...">
</head>
<body>
    <div class="container">
        <h1>Bitcoin Price Tracker</h1>
    </div>
    <script src="https://cdn.jsdelivr.net/npm/bootstrap@5.3.3/..."></script>
</body>
</html>
```

We will do a little mock Bitcoin Price Tracker app, that fetches from the server every five seconds.

In <body>, add the below markup:
```
...
<body>
    <div class="container">
        <h1>Bitcoin Price Tracker</h1>
        <h2 hx-get="/get-price" hx-trigger="every 5s">Loading...</h2>
    </div>
    ...
</body>
```

In our <h2>, we send a GET request to */get-price*. With **hx-trigger="every 5s",** the GET request will be triggered every 5 seconds.

We display "Loading…" to begin with.

Let's go to server.js and add:

...

36

```
...
let currentPrice = 60;

app.get('/get-price',(req,res)=>{
    currentPrice = currentPrice + Math.random() * 2 - 1;
    res.send('$' + currentPrice.toFixed(1))
})

// Start the server
app.listen (3000, ()=>{
  console.log('Server listening on port 3000');
});
```

We start off with a current price of 60 (current estimated price of bitcoin)

In *app.get('/get-price')*, to simplify things, I'm not going to actually reach out to a price API (although you could if you wanted to), but just generate a random price change with `currentPrice + Math.random() * 2 - 1`.

And with *res.send('$' + currentPrice.toFixed(1))*. We respond with the new price. We add *toFixed*(1) to have one decimal place and concatenate '$' before the price.

Running our App

So let's save, and in every 5 seconds, our app should make a new request to get the latest bitcoin price.

Bitcoin Price Tracker

$69.1

Obviously this isn't the real price because we're just simulating it. But you could connect this to a Bitcoin API if you wanted to, and you'd have updating of prices in real time.

Chapter 4: Building a Search Widget

Let's create a little search widget where we can search for users through an input text field, which fires off a POST request each time user types a key.

Save your index.html from the previous chapter and begin with a fresh new index.html that contains an input and a table to contain the results:

```html
<!DOCTYPE html>
<html lang="en">
<head>
    ...
</head>
<body>
    <div class="container">
        <h1>Search Users</h1>
        <input type="text"
            class="form-control"
            name="search"
            placeholder="Start Typing to Search for Users"
        >
        <table class="table">
            <thead>
              <tr>
                <th scope="col">First</th>
                <th scope="col">Last</th>
              </tr>
            </thead>
            <tbody>
              <tr>
                <td>Mark</td>
                <td>Otto</td>
              </tr>
            </tbody>
        </table>
    </div>
    <script ... ></script>
</body>
</html>
```
(table component taken from getbootstrap.com/docs/4.2/content/tables/)

This will get us something like:

Search Users

april

First	**Last**
Leanne Graham	Sincere@april.biz

We just have a container, an input and a table. We haven't added any HTMX attributes yet. We want to fill the table body with the results. So in table body, add in **bold**:

```
...
<table class="table">
    <thead>
      <tr>
        <th scope="col">First</th>
        <th scope="col">Last</th>
      </tr>
    </thead>
    <tbody id="search-results">
    </tbody>
</table>
...
```

The table body has an id of "search-results". That will be our target where we place the search results.

Next, let's go to the input and add in **bold**:

```
...
<h1>Search Users</h1>
<input
    type="text"
    class="form-control"
    name="search"
    placeholder="Start Typing to Search for Users"
    hx-post="/search"
    hx-trigger="input changed delay:500ms, search"
    hx-target="#search-results"
>
<table class="table">
    <thead>
...
```

Code Explanation

```
hx-post="/search"
```

We add *hx-post* to the input to make POST requests to '/search'.

```
hx-trigger="input changed delay:500ms, search"
```

We then add a trigger with *hx-trigger*. We specify "input changed" and also add "delay:500ms" to create a little delay of 500 milliseconds as users type (and we don't want to spam POST requests to the server!).

This will make a request each time we type something with a delay of 500ms in between.

```
hx-target="#search-results"
```

We specify *hx-target*, so the response will go to id of "search-results" which we have in the table body:

```
<table class="table">
    ...
    <tbody id="search-results">
    </tbody>
</table>
```

server.js

On the server side, in server.js, we add the 'search' route. So add:

```
// Handle POST request for contacts search
app.post('/search', async(req, res) => {

    const searchTerm = req.body.search.toLowerCase();
    if(!searchTerm) {
        return res.send('<tr></tr>');
    }

    const response = await
fetch(`https://jsonplaceholder.typicode.com/users`);
    const users = await response.json()
});
```

Code Explanation

```
app.post('/search', async(req, res) => {
```

We handle the post request '/search' for user search.

```
  const searchTerm = req.body.search.toLowerCase();
    if(!searchTerm) {
        return res.send('<tr></tr>');
    }
```

We retrieve the search term entered by the user *req.body.search* (input name is 'search') and assign it to *const searchTerm*. We set the *searchTerm* to lowercase so we don't have to worry about case-sensitive issues later.

We then check to see if there's no search term, we just return an empty table row. Otherwise, carry on to show all the users.

```
    const response = await
fetch(`https://jsonplaceholder.typicode.com/users`);
    const users = await response.json()
```

Next, we retrieve the list of users from JSONPlaceholder API as what we have done earlier.

Retrieve and Filter

Next, add in **bold**:

```
app.post('/search', async(req, res) => {
      ...

      ...
   const response = await fetch(`https://jsonplaceholder.typicode.com/users`);
   const users = await response.json()

   const searchResults = users.filter((user) =>{
       const name = user.name.toLowerCase();
       const email = user.email.toLowerCase();

       return name.includes(searchTerm) || email.includes(searchTerm)
   })

   const searchResultHtml = searchResults
       .map((user) => `
          <tr>
              <td>${user.name}</td>
              <td>${user.email}</td>
          </tr>
       `)
       .join('');
   res.send(searchResultHtml);
});
```

Code Explanation

```
const searchResults = users.filter((user) =>{
        const name = user.name.toLowerCase();
        const email = user.email.toLowerCase();

        return name.includes(searchTerm) || email.includes(searchTerm)
})
```

We perform a filter on the search results with the *filter* method. We say, for each user, we retrieve the name and email, and make both lowercase (since 'searchTerm' is lowercase too).

```
        return name.includes(searchTerm) || email.includes(searchTerm)
```

We then check if name includes the search term or if email includes the search term.

```
    const searchResultHtml = searchResults
        .map((user) => `
            <tr>
                <td>${user.name}</td>
                <td>${user.email}</td>
            </tr>
        `)
        .join('');
```

We then *map* through *searchResults* and say for each user, return a table row with user name and email.

We use *.join('')* to turn it into a string.

```
res.send(searchResultHtml);
```

Finally we send the *searchResultHtml* as response.

Running our App

All right, let's try it out. So when I search for 'biz', we get the list of users whose email contain '.biz'.

Search Users

biz

Name	Email
Leanne Graham	Sincere@april.biz
Kurtis Weissnat	Telly.Hoeger@billy.biz
Clementina DuBuque	Rey.Padberg@karina.biz

So it's a nice little real time search that displays relevant search results as users key in their search terms.

Chapter 5: Form Inline Validation

Let's do a project on inline validation where we want to validate a form's email address to make sure it's formatted correctly. We'll show the validation message directly under that input.

Again, let's start a fresh new index.html with a basic form from Bootstrap (https://getbootstrap.com/docs/5.3/forms/overview/):

```
<!DOCTYPE html>
<html lang="en">
<head>
    ...
    <script src="https://unpkg.com/htmx.org@1.9.12" ...>
    </script>
    <link href="https://cdn.jsdelivr.net/npm/bootstrap@5.3.3/...">
</head>
<body>
    <div class="container">
        <form>
            <div class="mb-3">
              <label class="form-label">Email address</label>
              <input type="email" class="form-control">
            </div>
            <div class="mb-3">
              <label class="form-label">Password</label>
              <input type="password" class="form-control">
            </div>
            <button type="submit" class="btn btn-primary">Submit</button>
        </form>
    </div>
    <script
src="https://cdn.jsdelivr.net/npm/bootstrap@5.3.3/...></script>
</body>
</html>
```

Email address

user2

Password

• • • • •

Submit

When the user types in the email and clicks outside or goes to another field, it should validate the email and highlight to the user if that email was valid or not.

Normally, we will have a *hx-post* on the form for the submission, but in this chapter, we are not really concerned with the submission. We will make a separate request to validate the email address.

So let's add in the input:

```
...
<form>
    <div class="mb-3">
        <label class="form-label">Email address</label>
        <input
          type="email"
          class="form-control"
          name="email"
          hx-post="/email"
          >
    </div>
...
```

We add *hx-post* and set that to */email*. Note that */email* is not for form submission, its just for the email field validation. When we type in the email field and click outside of it, it makes a request to */email* for the email validation.

Next, in the *div* above the email label, we add *hx-target="this"* and also *hx-swap* to "outer HTML":

```
...
<form>
    <div class="mb-3" hx-target="this" hx-swap="outerHTML">
        <label class="form-label">Email address</label>
        <input
          type="email"
...
```

45

We will get the HTML response from */email* that has a message indicating if it's a valid email or not, and use it to replace the whole div. We will come back to explaining this later.

For now, let's create the */email* route in our backend server.js. In server.js, add:

```
// Handle POST request for email validation
app.post('/email', (req, res) =>{
    const submittedEmail = req.body.email;
    const emailRegex = /^[a-zA-Z0-9._%+-]+@[a-zA-Z0-9.-]+\.[a-zA-Z]{2,}$/;
});
```

We first get the submitted email with *req.body.email*. Then, we use regular expression to match against to ensure the email is valid. The expression is a standard simple one that validates an email address.

Next, we do a test if the *submittedEmail* is valid. Add

```
app.post('/email', (req, res) =>{
    const submittedEmail = req.body.email;
    const emailRegex = /^[a-zA-Z0-9._%+-]+@[a-zA-Z0-9.-]+\.[a-zA-Z]{2,}$/;

    if(emailRegex.test(submittedEmail)) {
        return res.send(
            `...`
        )
    }
    else{
        return res.send(
            `...`
        )
    }
});
```

We use the *test* method and pass in *submittedEmail* to test it against the regex expression. If that's true, meaning, it's a valid email, we return *res.send* with backticks.

Remember that *res.send* will output a HTML response to replace the current whole *div* as shown in the square (this will become clearer later):

46

```
<body>
    <div class="container">
        <form>
            <div class="mb-3" hx-target="this" hx-swap="outerHTML">
                <label class="form-label">Email address</label>
                <input
                    type="email"
                    class="form-control"
                    name="email"
                    hx-post="/email"
                >
            </div>
```

So, add in **bold**:

...

```
app.post('/email', (req, res) =>{
    const submittedEmail = req.body.email;
    const emailRegex = /^[a-zA-Z0-9._%+-]+@[a-zA-Z0-9.-]+\.[a-zA-
Z]{2,}$/;

    if(emailRegex.test(submittedEmail)) {
        return res.send(`
            <div class="mb-3" hx-target="this" hx-swap="outerHTML">
                <label class="form-label">Email address</label>
                <input
                    type="email"
                    class="form-control"
                    name="email"
                    hx-post="/email"
                    value="${submittedEmail}"
                >
                <div class="alert alert-success" role="alert">
                    That email is valid
                </div>
            </div>`
        )
    }
    ...
```

Code Explanation

res.send will output all the current elements in the div i.e. the label, the input (we can just copy-paste from index.html). We also add to the input:

```
value="${submittedEmail}"
```

47

because we want the submitted email to stay in the input.

Under the input, we have the email valid message:

```
<div class="alert alert-success" role="alert">
    That email is valid
</div>
```

The "alert-success" class from Bootstrap show the message in a nice green color:
Email address

greglim@greg.com

That email is valid

Next, we do a similar thing in the *else* clause for an invalid email. You can copy and paste the above into the *else* clause:

```
app.post('/email', (req, res) =>{
    ...
    if(emailRegex.test(submittedEmail)) {
    ...
    }
    else{
        return res.send(`
            <div class="mb-3" hx-target="this" hx-swap="outerHTML">
            <label class="form-label">Email address</label>
            <input
                type="email"
                class="form-control"
                name="email"
                hx-post="/email"
                value="${submittedEmail}"
            >
            <div class="alert alert-danger" role="alert">
                Please enter a valid email address
            </div>
        </div>`
        )
    }
});
```

It's the same markup as the valid email except that for invalid email, we use the *alert-danger* Bootstrap class:

```
<div class="alert alert-danger" role="alert">
    Please enter a valid email address
</div>
```

Email address

123

Please enter a valid email address

Running our App

Let's reload and enter a valid email address:

Email address

greglim@greg.com

That email is valid

So it's just inserting this block of code:

```
// Handle POST request for email validation
app.post('/email', (req, res) =>{
    const submittedEmail = req.body.email;
    const emailRegex = /^[a-zA-Z0-9._%+-]+@[a-zA-Z0-9.-]+\.[a-zA-Z]{

    if(emailRegex.test(submittedEmail)) {
        return res.send(`
            <div class="mb-3" hx-target="this" hx-swap="outerHTML">
                <label class="form-label">Email address</label>
                <input
                    type="email"
                    class="form-control"
                    name="email"
                    hx-post="/email"
                    value="${submittedEmail}"
                >
                <div class="alert alert-success" role="alert">
                    That email is valid
                </div>
            </div>`
        )
    }
```

49

where we targeted it in index.html:

```html
<body>
    <div class="container">
        <form>
            <div class="mb-3" hx-target="this" hx-swap="outerHTML">
                <label class="form-label">Email address</label>
                <input
                  type="email"
                  class="form-control"
                  name="email"
                  hx-post="/email"

                  >
            </div>
            <div class="mb-3">
                <label class="form-label">Password</label>
                <input type="password" class="form-control">
            </div>
            <button type="submit" class="btn btn-primary">Submit</but
        </form>
    </div>
```

The same goes for an invalid email:

Email address

123

Please enter a valid email address

You could tweak this example to see if an email existed or not in the database. I hope these examples show you how HTMX works.

So again, we're dynamically replacing parts of our page without having to reload it and without using any JavaScript on the frontend.

Hopefully this gives you some insight on some of the reasons you would use HTMX.

Chapter 6: Show Edit Form and Update

In this chapter, we will illustrate a simple user profile that you can click to update. You click it:

Greg Lim

Follower of Christ | Author of Best-selling Amazon Tech Books and Creator of Coding Courses

Click To Edit

it's replaced with a form:

Name

Greg Lim

Bio

Follower of Christ | Author of Best-selling Amazon Tech Books and Creator of Coding Courses

Save Changes

and you can update and save your changes:

John Lim

Best Udemy Instructor

Click To Edit

We will have our index.html to show a simple user profile:

```
<!DOCTYPE html>
<html lang="en">
<head>
    ...
    <script
        src="https://unpkg.com/htmx.org@1.9.12"...>
    </script>
    <link href="https://cdn.jsdelivr.net/npm/bootstrap@5.3.3/...>
</head>
```

```
<body>
    <div class="container">
        <div class="card" style="width: 18rem;"
            hx-target="this"
            hx-swap="outerHTML"
        >
            <div class="card-body">
              <h5 class="card-title">Greg Lim</h5>
              <p class="card-text">
                Follower of Christ | Author of Best-selling Amazon Tech
Books and Creator of Coding Courses
              </p>
              <button href="#" class="btn btn-primary"
                hx-get="/user/1/edit">
                Click To Edit
              </button>
            </div>
        </div>
    </div>
    <script
src="https://cdn.jsdelivr.net/npm/bootstrap@5.3.3/..."></script>
</body>
</html>
```

The above will give you my user profile:

Greg Lim

Follower of Christ | Author of Best-
selling Amazon Tech Books and
Creator of Coding Courses

Click To Edit

Note: I am using the Bootstrap Card component
(https://getbootstrap.com/docs/5.3/components/card/)

Code Explanation

```
<div class="card" style="width: 18rem;"
    hx-target="this"
    hx-swap="outerHTML"
>
    <div class="card-body">
        ...
    </div>
</div>
```

We again use the *hx-target="this"* attribute to apply the changes from the response to the element itself. (*this* refers to the current HTML element, which is the <div class="card"> in this case). *hx-swap="outerHTML"* replaces the entire outer HTML of the target (the card itself here) with the response.

```
<button href="#" class="btn btn-primary"
  hx-get="/user/1/edit">
  Click To Edit
</button>
```

With *hx-get="/user/1/edit"*, the 'Click to Edit' button performs a GET request to the URL */user/1/edit* when clicked.

This fetches the user data with id '1' for editing in a form (implemented later).

Handling /user/:id/edit

We next implement the handler for the "/user/1/edit" route. In server.js, add:

```
// Handle GET request for profile edit
app.get('/user/:id/edit', (req, res) => {

    // send an HTML form for editing
    res.send(`
        <form hx-put="/user/1" hx-target="this" hx-swap="outerHTML">
            <div class="mb-3">
                <label for="name" class="form-label">Name</label>
                <input type="text" class="form-control" id="name"
```

54

```
name="name" value="Greg Lim">
            </div>
            <div class="mb-3">
                <label for="bio" class="form-label">Bio</label>
                <textarea type="text" class="form-control" id="bio"
name="bio">Follower of Christ | Author of Best-selling Amazon Tech Books
and Creator of Coding Courses
                </textarea>
            </div>
            <button type="submit" class="btn btn-primary">
                Save Changes
            </button>
    </form>
    `);
  });
```

(contact support@i-ducate.com for the source codes if you prefer to copy-paste)

Code Explanation

This would give us the editing form:

Name

Greg Lim

Bio

Follower of Christ | Author of Best-selling Amazon Tech Books and Creator of Coding Courses

Save Changes

```
    res.send(`
        <form hx-put="/user/1" hx-target="this" hx-swap="outerHTML">
        ...
        ...
        </form>
```

We dynamically serve an HTML form for editing the user profile based on the user ID specified in the URL */user/:id/edit*. Eg, /user/1/edit targets user with ID 1.

```
<input type="text" class="form-control" id="name" name="name" value="Greg
Lim">
    ...
<textarea type="text" class="form-control" id="bio" name="bio">
Follower of Christ | Author of Best-selling Amazon Tech Books and Creator
of Coding Courses
</textarea>
```

The form includes input fields pre-filled with existing values (values like "Greg Lim" are placeholders for actual data that should be fetched from a database). The user can then edit the fields:

Name

John Lim

Bio

Best Udemy Instructor

Save Changes

```
res.send(`
    <form hx-put="/user/1" hx-target="this" hx-swap="outerHTML">
    ...
    ...
    </form>
```

With *hx-put="/user/1"*, the form sends a PUT request to '/user/1'.

The response from the PUT request *hx-put="/user/1"* will be the updated user profile (implemented later) which would replace the current form on the page.

Let's now handle the PUT request *hx-put="/user/1"*

Handling PUT Request /user/:id/

In server.js, add:

```
// Handle PUT request for editing
app.put('/user/:id', (req, res) => {
  const name = req.body.name;
  const bio = req.body.bio;

  // Send the updated profile back
  res.send(`
      <div class="card" style="width: 18rem;"
          hx-target="this"
          hx-swap="outerHTML"
      >
          <div class="card-body">
              <h5 class="card-title">${name}</h5>
              <p class="card-text">
                  ${bio}
              </p>
              <button href="#" class="btn btn-primary"
                  hx-get="/user/1/edit">
                  Click To Edit
              </button>
          </div>
      </div>
  `);
});
```

Code Explanation

```
app.put('/user/:id', (req, res) => {
  const name = req.body.name;
  const bio = req.body.bio;
```

We handle the PUT request to update our user profile. We extract *name* and *bio* from the body of the request.

```
  // Send the updated profile back
  res.send(`
```

We then send the updated profile back to the client. You would typically update the data in a database (not shown in this code snippet but would typically be the case). We then respond with the updated user profile.

57

```
<div class="card" style="width: 18rem;"
    hx-target="this"
    hx-swap="outerHTML"
>
    <div class="card-body">
        <h5 class="card-title">${name}</h5>
        <p class="card-text">
            ${bio}
        </p>
        <button href="#" class="btn btn-primary"
            hx-get="/user/1/edit">
            Click To Edit
        </button>
    </div>
</div>
```

The response is the Card layout from index.html that displays the updated name and bio (so you can copy and paste from there). It includes the 'Click to Edit' button to trigger another edit if needed. We dynamically fill with the new values using JavaScript template literals ${name}, ${bio}.

John Lim

Best Udemy Instructor

Click To Edit

Overall, the HTMX attributes enhance our form by enabling it to fetch and display new/updated content directly within the form/card area without needing a full page reload. This makes the user interface more dynamic and responsive.

Cancel Button

Lastly, let's add a Cancel button to our Edit form in case the user wants to cancel the edit and return to the user profile page:

Name

Greg Lim

Bio

Follower of Christ | Author of Best-selling Amazon

Save Changes   Cancel

In server.js, add:

```
app.get('/user/:id/edit', (req, res) => {
    res.send(`
        <form hx-put="/user/1" hx-target="this" hx-swap="outerHTML">
            ...
            <button type="submit" class="btn btn-primary">
                Save Changes
            </button>
            <button type="submit" hx-get="/index.html"
                class="btn btn-secondary">
                Cancel
            </button>
        </form>
    `);
});
```

We add a Cancel Button with the HTMX attribute *hx-get="/index.html"*. Unlike the 'Save Changes' button, when clicked, 'Cancel' sends an HTTP GET request to /index.html to fetch index.html.

Summary

Hopefully, you have enjoyed this book and would like to learn more from me. I would love to get your feedback, learning what you liked and didn't for us to improve.

Please feel free to email me at support@i-ducate.com if you encounter any errors with your code or to get updated versions of this book.

If you didn't like the book, or if you feel that I should have covered certain additional topics, please email us to let us know. This book can only get better thanks to readers like you. If you like the book, I would appreciate if you could leave us a review too. Thank you and all the best!

About the Author

Greg Lim is a technologist and author of several programming books. Greg has many years in teaching programming in tertiary institutions and he places special emphasis on learning by doing.

Contact Greg at support@i-ducate.com